To the wonderful
Treiman Family —

With love and blessings!

Rose Taylor,

Santa Monica
april 7, 1986

900 Euclid St. (205)
S.M. 90403

POEMS

FOR

MY

PEOPLE

By the Same Author
Poems for My People, original edition, 1960
This Miracle, This Place, These Palisades, 1985

POEMS

FOR

MY

PEOPLE

ROSE TAYLOR

EUCLID PRESS

SANTA MONICA, CA.

1986

Dedicated to Maurie
and our children
Mady, Norman and David

ACKNOWLEDGEMENTS — 2nd EDITION

A note to David: You were only fifteen and in high school, and you gave up many Saturdays and holidays to print my book. How can I forget your joy in doing that; you came home on your bike, with the galley sheets tucked inside your jacket.

I am happy that Mady has read a number of the poems in her exercise classes; and now Heidi, my granddaughter, accompanies me on programs to give an actress' interpretation of my writing.

When the book appeared, who else but a Rabbi like Marvin Bornstein could read so beautifully on a special Sabbath in honor of its publication? And who else but those beautiful sisters - Pearl Esensten, Ida Fligsten, Sarah Collen, Edythe Karon, and their husbands, could be such magnificent hosts?

There were requests for the book from people like Dr. Abraham Kotsuji, a Japanese convert, for his Jewish Library in Kyoto; Marvin Bennett of KABC, who read many of the poems on two programs; Hannah Berman, who founded the Ross Taylor Literary Guild; · Dovid Mandell for whom the book was transcribed into Braille; a chaplain in Korea; gift shops at temples; Hadassah chapters in Montreal.

And thank you, Maurie, for all the years you accompanied me whenever I appeared on a program.

Rose Taylor

INTRODUCTION

A Hasidic sage taught: "If finding means an end of searching, it would be better to go on searching."

In Rose Taylor's verse, perhaps in all poetry, the quest itself becomes a goal and a fulfillment. With her, we explore nature's wonders, the American dream, the depths of grief, the heights of love. With her, we deny loneliness, extol courage, savor sweet and bitter memories of the Jewish past, and glory in the energy of Israel.

Some of her most appealing moments are precisely in the search for meaning in the familiar scenes and sounds of Jewish life: the Yiddish street, the Passover Seder, the day of the Bar Mitzvah, a small boy lighting a Chanukah candle.

Her tone is gentle, even when she challenges the skeptic or the non-observant: "Dear one, do not hesitate," she sings, "do not turn away/ we will greet you/ as a beloved brother ..."

And her quest can bounce with humor too, as in *When You Ask A Jew*, or *The Rebetzin*, who "may have beauty, but not be too beautiful..."

This collection brings us the harvest of years. As a friend, I find myself searching for the individuals whose faces reveal themselves in these verses. I found some of them. But then, remembering the old Rebbe's advice, I have to go back and search again. There's more here than the identity of a son or daughter.

So I welcome new readers to Rose Taylor's circle of friendship. Here you will hear echoes of cries and of laughter that may be your own. In her own words, she has given us all "soft music, to stir my soul/ my soul that is mute ..."
ENJOY!

Baruch Cohon

FOREWORD

In the Pirke Avoth (The Sayings of the Fathers), it is said, "He who learns from his fellow a single chapter, a single rule, a single verse, a single expression, or even a single letter, ought to pay him honor."

It is not "honor" that I want, but rather to know that one poem of mine — one line — one phrase even, will excite someone; that even the one word someone may need is in this book.

I first learned to love poetry when I was a small girl studying in the Yiddishe Folks Shule in Montreal. All of us learned to recite poems, and the recitation of poetry was one of the highlights of the yearly concerts.

I want to thank those who have clasped my hand when I finished reading my poetry; those who have even kissed me, and those who have listened as I poured out my songs as soon as I finished writing them.

My heartfelt thanks to friends who have shown a great interest in my writing: Bess Freeman, Sally Fineberg, Zillah Kohn, Deon Simon, Saralyn Winnick, Isabel Kagan, Tillie Mandel, Elfreda Tarler, Selma Heuer, Mabel Dokovna, Marie Hardy and I. Lechtman. A special mention: the late great S. Morgan Powell, Editor of the "Montreal Star," who was the first to publish my poetry; also my sister Dorothy Yane and my brother, Moishe Applebaum.

Rose Taylor

CONTENTS

America, Beloved Land

From seed of freedom
planted long ago,
abundant is our harvest now,
granting a blessed portion
to every human being
in this, our beloved land

Sacred is the parchment
wherein is written
this Declaration of freedom:
from tyranny
from oppression
from injustice

Consecrated are the
names of men
who would no longer suffer
humility
humiliation,
but who believed only
in a crown
every man could wear -
the crown of independence,
invisible, yet manifest
in the Rights of man,
attained only
by the righteous

Oh, America!
Land of kindred States,

unfurl your flag
With hand on heart,
with thankful eyes,
we gaze reverently
at this cloth of courage
and consecrate anew,
with faith and hope,
our allegiance
to this beloved,
beloved land

This My Land,
These My People

Come!
Let us drive
through scores of tiny towns
sleeping drowsily, contentedly,
under the hot, silver sun
while here and there
a ball of tumbleweed
slides lazily
through the dusty fields

See . . . those hills
softly beckoning
and the mountains,
blue and red and misty green

See that waterfall,
white and foamy,
gushing down the mountain side

See those groves
studded with pungent gold
of lemon and lime,
of orange and grapefruit
and the trees
laden with peppers,
glistening green,
more beautiful than jade

Behold the flowers
in this, my land

Look! there in the distance,
the horses . . . cattle
are grazing quietly on
the sloping grass

See this, my land
with its cactus and its scrub-lands
and lakes and rivers and mainlands.

Here, too, is the spell
of the mighty city,
beating with a strange,
steady rhythm
and the mammoth swish
of cars crunching on endless roads

Hear the machines set whirring
by tough-muscled men
see the steel mills' glowing fires
flashing day and night
and oil wells sucking liquid
from the very depths of earth
and stores burgeoning
with goods woven
from men's imagination

Homes, tree-sheltered,
nestle in their gardens
and buildings thrust boldly
toward the sky
see this, my land

See my people,
great in number are they,
warm and laughing,
swift with humor, jest,
poised for any challenge,
articulate,
fair and decent,
charitable

Many tongues you'll hear
beating 'neath one giant heart,
many shades of skin you'll find
and cultures, old and new,
from many lands they've come,
seeking freedom,
for the right to live
they've come

Let us sing!
Sing with one voice,
songs of joy and pride
for this, our land,
for these, our people!

I Am A Jew

I do not say this calmly, coolly . . .
no!
My blood is hot with this knowledge,
hot as the sand
in the land of Egypt
where my ancestors lived
and hot as the sun
that beat upon them in the desert

It is invisibly
sealed —
always, instinctively,
the thought is with me,
I am a Jew,
a link,
forged for eternity,
that binds me to my people
in every home and street and town,
in every city and every land,
every one of them!

Their burdens are my burdens,
their terror mine,
their tears,
their afflictions,
their defeats
are mine

And their glory is mine,
their pride,

their faith and strength,
their thirst for ever-widening
horizons of learning
their compassion,
their wit
and imperishable humor —
these are mine.

As it is written:
with every beat of my heart,
with every step I take,
when I sit
and when I walk;
when I lie down
and when I rise,
when I talk to my children
there is a continuing thread,
deeply, inextricably,
woven and interwoven,
I am a Jew

Across the hills and mountains,
across rivers and plains,
across desert,
in every spot
no matter if it is day or dark,
through rain and heat,
through snow and sleet,
there is no obstacle:
my words,

my heart,
my spirit,
all my senses
reach out to all my people!

Yiddish Street

Here, on this Yiddish Street,
I am at home
walking leisurely,
contentedly,
among my people,
smiling at everyone,
listening to the fragments
of conversation

The older folks
talk in Yiddish
some speak in broken English
with gestures, of course,
and where else
could their accent be more natural?

Here they don't know
about fancy displays.
The Grocery window is filled
with pumpkin seeds
and prunes
and apricots
and nuts
and bockser
and lima beans
and buckwheat groats,
and always you smell
the dill pickles . . .

The Bakery
beckons with its scent of
poppy seed and sesame,
the warm smell of bagel
and onion rolls.
The shelves are filled
with black and white
and brown breads,
shining, crusty, luscious —
round or long shaped loaves,
and the twisted challas,
and the queen of pastries,
shtrudel

The Book Store
is filled with things
dear to the Yiddish heart:
books
(every one of which
has been read by the
learned proprietor
in Hebrew, Yiddish or English)
candelabra,
ornate or simple
jewelry
Mogen Davids, some
infinitesimally small
and delicate;
Tefellin
Taleisim

Yarmelkas
Kiddish cups
Mezuzahs
and now
beautiful Israeli objects

Hear that man
speak of his merchandise
There is fire in his eyes
he is the happiest man in the world
who sells his fellow Jews
these symbols
of Judaism

Here you see grandparents
buying their grandson's
Tallis for his Bar-Mitzvah,
a mother choosing
a Menorah for her daughter,
a little Jew
stops in to buy
the Yiddish paper.
On the walls of the Book Store,
year after year,
like guardians,
hang awe-inspiring pictures
of old rabbis
forever immersed
in religious tomes

11

As you walk from store to store,
you hear the quickening sounds
of Israeli songs
from the Record Shop
and joy
enters your very blood-stream

In the Delicatessen
every seat is filled,
it is like a big happy family,
everyone eats with gusto,
no one worries
about being dainty
it's good to eat!

There is a potpourri
of tantalizing odors
oriental scent of halvah
mingling with the aroma of
hot pastrami,
cornbeef,
and pickled herring

And here on the Street
stand groups
of people talking,
laughing at some witticism,
staring curiously
at every passer-by

All Jews are drawn
to this Street,
this warmth,
this flavor.
This essence,
this sense of belonging,
you will find only
on the Yiddish Street

Shomrim

Forever they
guard us,
writing for us,
setting down every word
to remember
of the past, long long ago,
and now

Forever they
talk to us,
telling us not to forget,
repeating over and over
old stories,
and weaving in the new,
the tragedies
and happy endings,
centuries later

They never rest
wherever there is a Jew,
they go,
what does he need?
Every Jew is precious
and all his children must know
they are flesh and blood
of immortal heroes

They fight for us,
our Shomrim,
no matter who the enemy,

with tongue
and with rifle,
with money
and with blood

Shomrim,
we need you
We rely on you
It is you who are
the chosen people

What Is A Jew?

Yes, what is a Jew?

> He is not only
> that one killed savagely
> in pogroms
> thrown by the thousands
> into burning fires

He is not only
the one ostracized
held prisoner in ghettos
or banished from his country
ridiculed, humiliated

> He is not only
> the one who died of t.b.
> in the sweatshops

He is the reader
the learner
the writer
the thinker
the scientist
the composer the poet
and artist
the brilliant teacher

And he is the humorist
whose wit delights
and brings laughter

to the world
and whose genius
has kept his people alive
through the centuries:
so like the tiny flower
rising through rigid asphalt
into the light, the sunshine
strong, enduring
triumphant
forever

Ratio

What is the ratio of Man to Life?
The ratio of Happiness to Strife?

The answer, I know, can't be equal
Unless after life there's a sequel

Hearts may be torn with sighs and sorrow
Then mended with a smile tomorrow.

Boundless Is My Love

Boundless is my love for you,
limitless!
Vast, as the life-giving
system within me,
greater than any vista
the human eye can span

Boundless is my love for you,
limitless!
Secret as the source
of flower's scent;
imperceptible as the flutter
of the tiniest creature's
fragile wings,
constant as the tireless
sway of leaves in a breeze

Boundless is my love for you,
limitless!
I, who prayed for you,
cradled you weeks and days
and nights within my body,
was suddenly miraculous,
having borne you

Boundless is my love for you,
limitless!
and a prayer for you
pours from my heart
with agony, as at birth,

that you will be strong
and vital and compassionate
with a mind of depth,
yet clear as sky's reflection
in a lovely lake:
hearing all the world's sounds
throbbing throbbing

Oh, boundless, boundless,
is my love for you!
Limitless!
Limitless!

In The Garden

The earth is vibrant,
rich with all the riches
man needs, desires.
The earth is yielding, ripe,
the grass is tender,
the sun embraces
warmly, tenderly

Have faith!
Believe! Believe!

Note how the blossoms
drink of the gleaming dew
Note the grace of the bird
Feel the mystery of the night,
look upward to the golden stars
Sing to the glory of the day
with all its colors, odors

And always there is the child
sleeping trustingly,
dreaming, laughing,
shouting
exultant as the blood
courses joyously through
its young and oh so
beautiful body

And always there is the child
you love with boundless love,

so sleep trustingly,
exult with him,
dream with him,
laugh and shout

He has faith!
He believes!
He believes!

Only Once

You never wanted to be a Jew
there were so many things
that engrossed you

> But I know that if you will
> come to Shule
> only once —
> to hear *Kol Nidre*
> you will be a Jew

It Is My Life

Why do I go
to the Synagogue?
Who calls?
There is no sound,
no bell tolls
again and again and again

Why do I go
to the Synagogue?
Why do you ask?
Is it not because
of the words of wisdom,
because of the chants
and prayers
and songs
and sounds
that draw me there?

Why do I go
to the Synagogue?
What do I see?
I look at the
Eternal Light
that sends a quiver
of joy through me

The opening of the Ark
is a precious mystery
unfolding that which
is the word of God

Ah, why do I
go to the Synagogue?
Do I not hear my father
and his father
and all those before me
pray and plead
and sing with ecstasy
to our Creator?

And I go to stand
side by side
with Jews,
to let our voices mingle,
to recite Kaddish with them,
to rejoice in the birth
of a new Israelite,
to see the proud Bar-Mitzvah
and those who cherish him,
to witness the betrothal
of young lovers,
to see a man and his beloved
become one under the chuppah

Why do I go to the Synagogue?
It is the Jewish way
It is my way
It is my life!

To A Young Girl

What will you remember
of your childhood?
Is it fear of the unknown?
the pain of disappointment
in a fallen idol?
sadness at disloyalty
where faith was placed?

Will you remember the cold,
when it was glowing warmth
and sweetness that you sought?

Will you remember the image
of the hard and tight-lipped,
the unseeing, into whose eyes
you gazed with passion, longing,
praying for response,
a nod of recognition?

Yes . . . yes . . .
these you will remember:
the relentless, the unforgiving,
the prying, the cruel

And oh yes, against your will,
you will remember
your frantic quest for love
and happiness,
your endless questioning,
never, never answered;

the trying . . . and the crying . . .
the searching . . . only to be pierced
like the thousand points
of splintered glass

But oh, my child,
there are the answers;
there are the people:
when first you seek
within yourself,
when first you come to those
who gave you life

A Jewish Woman

Before our eyes
she grows,
gaining knowledge
from her rabbis,
spurred on by them
to study books of wisdom,
Torah, Judaism's crown

Before our eyes
she grows,
speaking wondrously
from the depth of
her love for Judaism;
inspiring those who listen
with the glow and light
of her spirit

Before our eyes
she grows,
adorning every place
she enters,
beautifying every thing
she touches,
seeking in everyone
the greatest good;
magnifying the essence of
every thought and act

You cannot take her measure
for before our eyes

she grows,
every word ringing
with awe
of all the wondrous
things created,
of all the fine and beautiful
things to be created

The Rebetzin

She must be a diplomat
of great polish, the rebetzin,
and to know every turn of phrase
to be used when,
a greeter par excellence,
leaving no one out,
no matter how great the crowd,
nor forgetful of face or name . . .

> She may have beauty,
> but not be too beautiful;
> have poise, but just enough;
> be charming to every man,
> woman and child, no matter
> if her back aches
> or her feet hurt
> or she feels a cold coming on . . .
> she is a rebetzin
> and knows she must try
> to please everyone

> > They say it's hard to be a Jew
> > but it's harder to be a rebetzin

Sabra

Sabra,
beautiful Sabra!
Who are you?
Our hearts quicken
at the sight of you;
our hearts are full
of love
when we behold you;
our hearts are full
of wonderment
when we behold you

Who are you,
Sabra,
with your fluid limbs
and supplicating hands?
Every movement,
every expression,
has been moulded, distilled,
into poetic perfection,
ineffable art

Who are you,
Sabra?
As you dance
with joyful pride,
fierce abandonment,
we echo
your stamping feet,
your clapping hands,

we stroke your
tousled, silken hair

Your music stirs
every cell within us;
vibrates . . .
until we are torn apart!
With throbbing throat
we hear your songs
of love and laughter,
of sand and sweat,
of a hero's death . . .
and tears
fall from our eyes
as we gaze on you,
Israeli girl,
glowing,
magnificent
Sabra!

Essence of wind and ice,
fire and blood,
flows in your veins!
You know well the biting frost,
clawing hunger,
choking thirst,
torture in boats beaten
by ocean's cruelty;
craftiness of the city,
and bitterness
of the closed-in village

And the story
of your shining strength,
sweet spirit,
resounds in the world
raising the hope
of all Jews,
filling all who see you,
with matchless admiration,
and silent blessings:
Sabra!
Sabra!

Niddah And Taharah

The rabbi from Europe
was not happy,
not happy at all,
with his congregation
in America,
they were not observant Jews,
they were not pious enough

So he wrote books
about the wisdom and beauty
of Judaism
and the health laws of
Niddah and Taharah

I went to the Mikvah,
my finger-and-toenails
devoid of polish,
my hair washed
and my body cleansed

I stepped into the hot, pure water
submerging myself three times,
and when I arose breathlessly,
the old woman who supervised
these proceedings
placed a lace kerchief
on my head
and blessed me
in Hebrew

"Tochter," she pleaded
in Yiddish,
pressing my arm,
"Tell the women
about this,
tell them!"

The Poet

She sits in reverie
her eyes reflect a thousand dreams
she holds her head with slender hands
as if it were an offering

The Sculptress

For many many years
      faintly . . . faintly . . .
these faces fluttered
in her memory

Until at last, miraculously,
vision, genius, fused
to give birth to beauty

      With hands and eyes,
      with love,
      with wisdom,
      she shaped those faces,
      each feature,
      each figure evoked
      with life-like clarity

      Whose . . . whose
      are those faces?

They are the faces of Jews,
forever old, forever new:
      the loving Zaide,
      Einikel, Gabbai,
      the Schneider and
      the Chosin-Kalle;
A proud procession of them,
immortal now
      The Rebbe,
      the Yeshiva Bocher,

        the Pastach,
            among many, many
and the heart throbs
when eyes behold
the ageless figure
            Mother Bencht Licht

And we?
We bless you, Sculptress,
we bless your hands,
we bless your heart
and we thank you

A Poem For Marcia

As it is written:
These words are
indelibly inscribed
on your heart
igniting you
impelling you
to seek
the words of Jewish women
written through the ages
which must be saved
and cherished

As you read,
your glowing face
and shining eyes
bring these treasures
to life,
revealing the writers', poets'
hearts and souls and minds:
their feelings flow
through your veins
and ours
as you project
your love

And we who listen
enter your precious circle
and share these words

So Rare

Woman of dark eyes
and olive skin

Your home
is like open arms,
inviting us to share
your food and warmth
and doing, going, bringing,
showing, giving

Your soul has come
from heaven
and rests in you,
a rare Nishamah

A Woman Prays

She prays,
her hands
lifted in supplication

She prays,
her face
serene,
etched with certainty
that God will listen

She prays,
her eyes are closed
and in the stillness of the room
all hearts mingle,
all hearts listen
and respond

In the still
soft-lighted room
she prays

Her Face

I can't forget her face

There is no Mona Lisa
passive look there,
only a radiant smile
that encompasses
everything and everyone
within her aura

And yet, one day
I saw the numbers stamped
upon her arm
and knew
from whom
from where
they came

I can't forget her face

Plea For Peace

All that I have been,
all that I am,
all that I will be,
I offer
for the sake of peace

My weapon
will be the words I speak,
the song on my lips
telling of man's frailty,
his struggles
his aspirations,
his charity,
his quivering,
passionate
love of life
with only a minute
portion of joy

I tell you:
My eyes I will lend
to all of you
and even your little ones,
telling them to see,
just to see!
To look!
Look!

My ears I will lend
to hear

(it takes a lifetime to hear)
sounds:
the sounds of water, wind
sounds:
music,
laughter,
your own joyous breath,
the beat of your heart
voices!

Oh, friend,
whatever is mine
I will share with you
at all times,
in all seasons.
This is my plea:
let us work together,
let us live in peace

Oh, man, if you will
see and hear,
if you will
look into my eyes
and listen,
you will never lift
your hand against me!

Warsaw Ghetto

I do not think of you
as dead,
as vanquished.
Though you died,
you won your siege
for freedom

Great, great,
and greater, will be
every act, every deed
uncovered of your
Maccabean courage

It is too late
for tears.
To keep
our sanity
we hold
Memorial Services,
we must talk
and light candles

Children Of Israel

You swim and play and romp
you study
you laugh and sing
your loveliness
is so endearing

But when you stop and pose
we see a new child
hand on hip
a certain stance
head held high
eyes steady, unflinching
you are the invincible
gallant children of Israel

Land Of Israel

Bare and desolate places,
you flourish now
with strata of flower
and grass
and full stout trees
that bear testimony
to the sweat-filled
years of labor

> Miles of precious
> pipe bring water
> to the hard dry earth,
> giving sustenance and life
> and the green of growth

> More and more
> of your waste land
> blooms
> from the toil
> and from the blood and will
> of Israel's
> blessed
> men and women

Golda Meir

You are a gift
to the Jewish people,
Golda Meir

    Who can assess
    the magnitude of your vision,
    for is it not distilled
    from times long past
    and ages yet to come?

Where comes your matchless power
if not from those
who knew no fear,
who scorned all threats,
who led our people
out of bondage
to victory
time and time again

    That face! Unforgettable!
    whose supreme purpose
    does not waver for an instant
    that voice, so vibrant
    reaches the hearts of millions

    What is one to say
    in the light of such greatness,
    divinely bestowed,
    except to say:
    You are a gift

to the Jewish people,
Golda Meir
and we glory
in your light

Return To Israel

There is no lament,
my friend,
because you leave,
no tears,
no sadness

Oh, would that I
too could travel
to the land
for which the heart yearns;
to see the blueness
of the sky
and the velvet gleam
of jewelled star

To walk on hills,
and gaze at valleys
where trod the noblest
of the noble;
to listen to your soul's
own tongue;
to see the faces
from myriad places
of the world,
streaming forever
to this land

Not only this
beckons you:
the beauty, warmth

the laughter and loveliness,
the ecstasy of home-coming,
But all the rest:
the toil,
and terror perhaps,
the need to do your share

There is no lament,
my friend,
because you leave
there is only the hope
for your health,
the wish for your happiness
in the land of our birth,
in the land of Israel!

A Tribute — David Ben Gurion

David Ben Gurion!
Blessed, hallowed,
be your name,
name of prophetic portent,
heroic destiny

David Ben Gurion!
Leading star of Zion,
you shine your benign light
on all Israel

Your voice is a clarion call
for men who sweat and strive
to fullfill their dreams,
for men who join in
selfless toil and labor
for our land

We want to make a pledge
to you forevermore:
we will take heed
of what you say,
we will keep sacred
that which you have written,
we will remember your words
pulsating with the rhythm
of your life's blood!

Your utterances,
ineffable, majestic,

will become a bond
of our heritage

We pledge to remember
the divine spirit
of courage
which you kindled
in every Jewish heart

Your true worth
is cherished now,
your exalted stature
will grow through
the centuries

We pray for peace,
Ben Gurion,
life's most precious jewel;
with humility
we pray for peace:
for you,
for Israel!

Those You Chose In the Kibbutz

These you chose,
to these you were drawn irrevocably
and more than that,
your soul responded
to a people
with a passion for learning,
with ideals for justice, peace
sensitivity to his brother's needs

    This way of life
    you chose:
    to sweat in labor,
    to match this people's will
    tangible with
    stratum upon stratum
    of indelible deeds,
    to fight their fights
    to sing their songs
    listen to their words
    eat and sleep with them,
    and always to marvel
    at the certainty
    of their goal
    their dream
    that must be attained,
    fulfilled

These you chose,
offering yourself,
every atom of your being,

for this purpose

These you choose,
there you live,
in the everlasting beauty
of the land
of your people

Wall Of Healing:
Hadassah Hospital, Israel

Always there will be a hospital
its name Hadassah
place of mercy,
healing!
No tyrant's evil
nor human force
will ever stop this from being so
or close its open door

Always Hadassah's plan
and dynamic dream
will survive
Always there will be this haven,
this unswerving will
to serve humanity

Road Of Valor — Israel

No other name could suit
this road,
made forever glorious
by its defenders

> There is no flag
> nor stone
> nor special mark
> to serve as history
> of this battle

> > Only the shattered parts
> > of ambushed trucks
> > remain as reminders
> > mute memento
> > of the struggle
> > for this road

> > > Though many fell,
> > > still their valiant spirit
> > > hovers here,
> > > on this Road of Valor

Through The Ages

Grasp my hand,
look at me,
I yearn for you, my children,
I yearn for you

Through the ages,
I have yearned for you
through war and terror
through famine and disease
through death and through fire
through all the ills that
have befallen you, my children,
I have yearned for you,
I have yearned for you

What can I give you, my children?

Love I will give you,
and peace.
What can I give you, my children?
I will give you the bluest
blue of Israel's sky,
I will give you its hot sands
and green trees,
I will give you its rain,
and the warmth of its sun will shine
upon white and brown and black

I will give you the sound
of the sea,

and the singing
of chalutzim,
I will give you
the wisdom
of bearded old Jews

You will hear the zestful sound
of your young,
the confident step
of your brave shomrim.
The whole world will listen
to your songs and sweet music,
and your buildings
will stand proud
on happy streets!

What can I give you, my children?

As a mother gives,
so I want to give
you the gift
above all other gifts,
life itself!
And peace, peace . . .
That soft, beautiful word:
shalom, shalom, shalom

After Writing "Through The Ages"

I wept
for I knew not how
I could write it

I wept,
the hot fluid
of my tears staining,
mingling
with the words
on paper

Oh, Israel
for you
flow these tears,
for you,
from whom we spring;
for all Jews
who work and dream,
endlessly,
timelessly,
for a golden circle
of nations,
speaking the language of
brotherhood,
harmony,
understanding,
and the ultimate goal,
of peace . . .

This poem of love

is for you,
for you,
Israel!
For your immortal poets
and dauntless fighters,
for every man
and woman
and child
to whom your name is
a symbol of our unity

I Won't Ask God

You think,
you brood,
the bitterness
never leaves you:
you ache,
you ask:
What of the Six Million . . .
How could it be,
how?

Mothers and fathers,
brothers and sisters,
children, infants,
old men,
old women,
the strong and the weak;
the helpless,
the trusting,
all were slaughtered,
all,
all Six Million
were slaughtered

Only the hands of a few,
so few,
futile as a butterfly,
were raised
to beat off
the murderous tread
of the enemy

Of all the words
that man can utter;
of all the words
of human tongue,
there is not one word
to explain this deed of deeds

The world's heart
was frozen
in some monstrous floe,
unable to beat,
to feel,
to rally,
while swiftly our people
were exterminated

Horror of horrors
were perpetrated,
beatings, burnings,
gas chambers,
the ghetto and the bunkers,
death from starvation,
suicide

Add yet this, yet this
to the bloody history
of our people,
and weep — weep — weep
if you can:
but never forget!
Never . . . never!

Echoes

Give me
soft music to stir my soul
my soul that is mute

Give me
your song, melodious and sweet,
to enter my heart

And I,
dear, will echo the beauty
your music has sent

A Small Bud Rising

You sit in the warm sun
and every fiber within
quivers with longing —
what, it is hard to say!
And you watch the earth's
creatures nearby going simply
about their business.
A black dishevelled caterpillar
crawls along calmly,
his destination is a spot
underneath a bush of red camellias.
It's odd to see a pinprick
of an ant
chugging along
on the concrete walk
(how many such ants
does one step on!)
Flies in the sun
are fun to watch,
it's only when there's food
that they're a nuisance!
Yet I have a new respect
for flies,
for once I saw a merry fly
perch himself on a cherry pit,
thrown away,
and dance on it!

What you write is
really not important,

but you want to set down in writing —
the wonder of the day,
quite an ordinary day
(or is it!)
yet the gentle chirp
of a bird,
the sound of sprinklers
splashing on the grass,
the whirr of cars,
all, all, all this,
makes me happy!

Even the labored,
thundering roll
of a plane's motor
is a part of the day.
Near the wall
pink roses grow,
my breath is caught
at one lone twig
with a small bud
rising high and proud
above the bush!

Nearby you hear
a child's voice
calling urgently:
"Mother! Mother!"
And I wish . . .
I wish . . .

I could call
my Mother . . .

Your Golden Wedding

Dearest Parents:
So long ago you met!
One, shy, trembling,
only a slight girl —
grey-eyed, tender-mouthed,
with blueblack hair, soft
and silken as a baby bird's breast,
with skin pink and glowing
as the sunset of a summer sky,
and hands of purest gold

The other:
a youth!
Eager, dark,
hair thick and curling
on the white brow;
swift in thought, witty,
decisive, emphatic,
never waiting passively,
but railing at the
infamous, the false;
swift with pity
in one's plight;
ofttimes reaching out, out
to the world,
for what he himself knew not.

Ah, 'tis good that life
moves swiftly
with its ever-changing panorama:

darkness and light,
happiness and frustration:
yet was hope surely beating
in your breast
with every sight of dawn,
every smile of child,
every affirmation of friendship,
with fiercest pride in your people,
your land's return

In youth
your children did not give
you time for sighing,
only time for working,
your hands never stopping
through the hours and days,
never halting
through the weeks and months,
nor ceasing now, thank God,
at the gold half-century.
Your gentle hands now
stroke a grandchild's head,
your hands are now for giving

Through the years
there was no bemoaning
the hardships,
nor complaining of fate.
Ever in your heart was
trust in God,

faith in man,
belief in goodness, truth.

God blessed you abundantly,
favoring you wih children
of worth
grandchildren, sweet and dear,
a golden great-grandchild.
May all of them be forever
a blessing unto you,
unto all mankind,
granting their love
abundantly,
as you have done,
giving of themselves
with your selflessness,
remembering you always,
cherishing you always!

To A Hero

You did not want to be a hero,
to wear a uniform
and march with pack
upon your back
and trudge through mud
nor crawl in dirt

Oh, my son,
what were you?
Just a boy,
thinking, dreaming,
running, laughing,
with sister, brother,
shyly dancing with a
sweet young girl

Because you did not want
to be a hero,
this you were:
greater, grander,
than any man,
you who hated war
and bloodshed,
you who never even threw
a pebble into water
fought to free your land,
your home

Oh, my son,
what were you?

Just a boy,
whistling, singing,
swimming in the rippling
water,
hiking on the hills,
gazing at sky and bird
Rushing eagerly,
with outstretched hands,
with confidence,
head-on,
to meet life.

But this I know,
you did not want
to be a hero

I Think Of Home

Again, now —
yet again, now
there is
the sharpness,
the insistent, persistent
sharpness
of my yearning,
my burning yearning
to see you
to see you
to be home!

With the fierceness
of the fiercest wind!
With the crash
of loudest thunder!
Like the splashing of
a downpour,
a deluge!
So is my need
to see you
to see you
to be home!

What is the fury
of whirling waters
in a storm?
Or the ceaseless beating
of a bird's wings
high above the earth?

Or the thousand wheels
of trains clacking
swiftly in the night
(going where . . . where . . .)
to the anguish I feel,
the bitterness,
hopelessness . . .
of not seeing you,
of not being home!

And I cannot tell you!
I cannot tell you!
Or . . . do you know?

In Memoriam — Ma

For the dreams
you never realized for me,
I cry!

For the things
I wanted to do for you,
but never did,
I cry

For the lovely things
you wanted
when you were young
but didn't have,
I cry

For all the places
yet to see,
for everything
you yearned to do,
I cry

For the need to
hear your voice
and laughter,
the ache
to see your face,
I cry

But most of all,
I cry
for the love
I felt
but didn't show

Mother

You will go quietly
by yourself
and cry,
and each tear will be
like a stone
dropping on your heart

You will remember
how she stood
in awe and said
"Oh, how beautiful
the sky is!"
She who loved
every living thing,
every bit of green,
every shape of flower,
every verdant thing

Ah, her voice
was so melodious,
each word was filled
with her mother love,
her mother care,
her mother heart

So much, so much,
we loved you!
No kiss, no word
could tell you
Perhaps you knew

Rest now, our dearest
treasure,
whose riches you bestowed
upon us
for so long,
yet you went too soon,
too soon

Oh, Ma Oh, Ma!

Every part of me trembles
when I remember this tableau
as we, her children,
stepped out of the car.

She stood a moment
and gazed upward
and we, sensing something
strange,
looked at her . . .

It was a warm summer night . . .
sundown, the sky blue-gray

She stood still
and uttered the last
words of her life:
        "Ah," she whispered,
        The sky is so beautiful."

. . . Separation, yes
sometimes it must be so

        But mothers should never die
        Oh, mothers should never die

Ma . . . Again

She is not here
her face I cannot see
nor touch her hand
yet every moment I know
that we are one,
just as when
I heard her heart beat,
nourished by
her veins and arteries,
alert to every thought she had
through the miracle
of our inter-communication system

> Every dream she had,
> I felt
> her every need,
> I yearned to fill

And though I groped
along the way
so many things I couldn't say
she too must have felt
that the cord, thank God,
was strong
and though invisible,

like a magnet
kept us aware
with every sense
forever drawn to one another
forever remembering

Bobbe

She sits on the porch
and breathes gently
of the summer air,
her eyes delighted with the
big old tree, the sky
with traces of tiny clouds
and children playing in the street

Yet now there is time to sit
she reflects sadly
how in the early days
everything revolved around her
"Ma! Ma! Bobbe! Bobbe!"
and she sits and remembers
and now she knows those years
were the best years of all

Challa

When she saw me
she said
I have a challa for you
I thought you'd like to have one

    She bakes challas
    for her family
    and makes enough for friends:
    If she had said
    I have a diamond for you
    I could not have been more happy

So much of her love
was in that loaf of bread
what were her thoughts
as she kneaded the dough
and saw it rise
and tenderly, carefully placed it
in the oven

    Did she remember
    all the Yom Tovs
    with her family
    everyone stopping first
    in the kitchen to
    kiss her pink perspiring cheek
    and then to taste
    the knaidlach and the knishes

Did she remember
the laughter, the news, the talk,
the special family jokes

What would Yom Tov
be without her challa,
golden-crusted
with its own delicious smell

What would Shabbos
be without her challa
or a simcha

Ah, dear friend,
I too have memories
as I eat your bread,
perhaps it is a symbol
of all I loved
in childhood

And it is an eternal symbol
that unites Jews everywhere
when we break bread together

They Live

There is a deep rent
in our hearts
when they pass,
those whom we love,
we want to cry,
we want to lament

There is a gash, a wound,
that never heals
when they pass,
those whom we love

There is a space within us
forever open to deeper hurt
when we remember
their beauty,
their nobility,
their utter sweetness
all encompassing
embracing all men,
every living thing

Yet with time, their memory
creates within us
greater strength,
finer understanding,
swifter sympathy

And though they pass
they live within us,
their breath forever
in our breath,
their blood forever
in our blood

A Certain Mood

Do not pity my loneliness
for I am never alone,
the slightest sound
brings me a message,
I sense what people feel,
I know what they think,
even if they pass my window.
The music a young girl plays
tells me if it is love she seeks
or gaiety and dancing
she yearns for

What is happening to people
is close to me,
people of endless variety:
the college graduate
in cap and gown
with his triumphant smile;
a grandmother, with her
proudest possession,
an infant's picture

The writer, the actor,
the builder,
everyone —
the ill, the weak,
all, all are close to me

Do not pity my loneliness
for I am never alone.

The very air you breathe,
others breathe;
the things you see
others also see.
The water you drink
quenches not only your thirst
and the food that gives you life
nourishes others too

And you remember
every handclasp in your life,
every kiss, every smile;
you remember not only
those who loved you
but you cannot ever forget
people you never met,
who lived and died
for you

Release

You strain
to explain
the words,
the thoughts trickling
through heart and mind,
like blood from a wound,
and you taste only salt

Alone,
you cannot unlock,
unfold,
chained-in senses,
feelings —
never, never alone

Joy evades
your outstretched
pleading hands
Success is pinned back
by a distant cloud
obscuring your sun
and love goes begging
like a lone little ant
zig-zagging in his search

Only when there is another
can you have release:
life, strength, success, joy!
And better yet
are many,

loving, sharing, caring,
responsive to
a touch, a glance,
a word, a thought

In Appreciation

Steppes, meadows, lanes and brooks,
vistas of untouched heaven
and earth
are my books

Powerful waves that urge to live,
a new awakening of hushed dreams,
or the soothing song of a lullaby
are my books

    Each one a treaure
    Each one a pleasure

Exaltation

O Lord, I thank Thee
for this beautiful day!
For the sun-warmed air I breathe
for the music that is in the wind
and children's laughter,
clear and sweet
like happy birds

I am one with this day
and my lips tremble with love:
O, Great Power!
O, Mighty Understanding!
Whence comes this feeling I have?
Who sent it to me?

I take this, my love,
and scatter it in the wind,
the love for men and women
and children,
oh, especially children,
with their eager eyes, pink lips
and trusting hands

Oh, my love!
Soothe the ill with gentle hands
and smooth their eyelids
that they may sleep,
dry the tears of those who weep

Oh, my love,
take these, my tears,
that fall steadily like rain
for all the world's pain
and melt all that's mean away

Oh, my love!
Open wide the windows
of the world:
let the sounds of the wind
in the branches
enter the walled rooms,
and the prayers of saints,
and the holy wisdom
of your wise men

O, Great Power!
O, Mighty Understanding!
Take this, my love!
Take this, my love!

Somewhere . . . Always

Please God,
let me remember
that somewhere, always,
there is suffering, want,
sickness, despair;
somewhere, always,
there is need to help,
to console,
to comfort,
to satisfy thirst,
hunger, love

Please, God,
let me remember
that somewhere — always,
there is hatred
dulling the soul,
numbing the mind,
pricking daily like the
ticking of a clock
or relentless click
of a monstrous metronome

Please, God
let me remember
there is hatred
between kings and kings,
between heads of state,
between man and man,
woman and woman.

Hatred:
scorching, searing,
scarring mankind
with its venom
hatred:
maiming, mutilating,
killing our young men,
crushing our daughters,
dealing a death sentence
to our mothers, fathers

But most of all,
please God,
let me not forget
there is love, benevolence,
warmth and tenderness,
pity and faith,
charity and forgiveness,
mercy,
saintliness.
Please, God, let me not forget
that somewhere — always —
there is love!

Description Of A Home

I know
it's not a humble place,
my home,
but certainly it's not a palace,
an estate, or mansion.
It is a home,
simply,
with just what one needs,
a few chairs and lamps and tables

No smart fabric
drapes our windows ,
no rugs still
the sound of shoes
on bare wood

Yet what makes this
a special place?

A nosy avocado tree is spreading,
spreading, its greedy branches
till it is almost
in my kitchen

The sloping lawn
is tidily marked off
by a white picket fence;
a trellis, somewhat tired,
balances bushes
where pink roses bloom

This I look at from my window,
from other windows
I can see tall pines
and hibiscus blooming

Others lived in this house
before me:
they planted lemons
and guavas
and plums
and grapes
and peaches
and apricots
and strawberries

I hear they loved this house;
they planted flowers too —
roses, gardenias, camellias,
iris, and many shrubs.
The air is filled
with this scent

This is a Jewish home.
On the Sabbath
I bless the candles.
Wine fills the gleaming
silver cups for the Kiddush.
We celebrate the holidays,
perhaps not so much in deed
as in knowing the meaning
of the days

And more than all
this is the place
where we play
and pray,
sleep, dream,
laugh or cry
together —
the family

Explanation

You say I'm cold — unyielding,
that my eyes are hard
and that my lips are primly set,
But do you understand?

Have you seen me gaze
up at the sky
in ecstasy,
or seen me, hushed and humble,
listen to the rustling leaves,
a symphony, a waterfall?

Have you seen me lost
in wonderment
before great paintings,
lovely poems,
the things you say?

You will never, never know
how warm and tender I can be
until I love you,
until you need me

Is There No One To Listen?

Is there no one to listen
when the heart weeps
with pain,
with pent-up sorrow,
longing?
If not, then this
I understand

But is there no one to listen
to your soaring ecstasy?
Your exquisite joy?
Your heart's utterances?
Is there no one, no one
to listen
to your song?

Spring Song

When you return
when you return
I will not speak,
I will offer you my lips
and the look in my eyes
and my body,
bathed in blossom scent

There will be yellow
candles burning,
and flowers
in every room,
I will wear
a flower in my hair
and will you tell me
that you care
when you return . . .
when you return?

And Now In November

I have had to part
with days
of precious sight and sound
and nights of stirring
scent and star

I have had to part
with your
love-conveying arms and eyes
and voice
so reverent and low
before the wonders of the world

And now
great tears of rain
beat down upon the earth,
the sharp-knifed wind
has cut down every leaf,
twig and trunk and branch of tree
are nets that wait for snow

For Your Sake

For your sake I would be beautiful,
not with milk-and-honey prettiness
to please the eye,
but with beauty that glows
like fireplace warmth
on a winter day

For your sake I would shine
like the rays of the sun
or like the quiet gleam
of moon and stars

For your sake I would sing
with the lusty lilt of lakes,
for your sake I would walk
with step as lithe as lilies

For your sake I would be wise,
not with the wisdom
of witty sayings,
but the wisdom to act
when action speaks,
and the silence that is more
spell-binding than any speech

For your sake I would be good,
not with the goodness
of advertised donations,
but with the goodness that
shares and helps and understands

For your sake I would be humble,
not with the humility of the meek,
but the humility of the loving
and the loved

There Are No Words

All sign of summer's passed
with all its loveliness
of fragrant flowers,
tender winds,
round gold moons
and stars and stars and stars,
and lying in your arms at midnight
upon the soft green hills

And though you did not speak
of love and love and love,
I do not care
there are no words so sweet
as the sweetness
of kisses and caresses;
there is no cup to measure
the brimming heart,
no meter for the beating pulse

My Song

Why do you say
I have not lived
because I sing
so lightly?

Would you say that of the
wind, the grass?
Would you say that of a
leaf, a twig?
Would you say that of a bird
in flight?
I ask: have you the right?

And would you say they have
not lived,
the inarticulate,
who span so much
in a mammoth moment?
Would you say they have
not lived?

It seems to me
that usually
they talk of living
who have not lived

I say only this:
I have been born
and reborn many times
and so long as there is

breath in me
I shall live
AND SING! AND SING!

II

My song was not meant for books,
held tightly shut between stiff
white sheets
and set sedately in square
black blocks,
then sniffed at by some solemn
critic,
who says, "She has not lived."

'Twas meant to be as free
as a bit of a breeze
on the tip of a tree

'Twas meant to seek
an eagle's nest,
a mountain peak

It is a message of love
on the warm wing of a dove

Every nerve and gland,
every throb of pulse,
is a tautened string
that makes my song ring

And if no one else

will listen,
I'll be content
to sing my song
near a sleepy stream,
a lonesome creek,
or close to a baby's
satin cheek

Nu, Tell Me

They say
it's hard to be a Jew:
Nu, tell me
if you're a Jew
can you be anything else?

They say
a leopard
never changes its spots

With a Jew
it's harder —
as a matter of fact
IMPOSSIBLE

Because you cannot
change your heart
your soul
your spirit

    Ah, yes
    once a Jew
    always a Jew:
    TRUE!

L'Chayim

As the dew on the grass
toasts the earth
refreshing it, giving it life
I too feel thankful
as I eat and drink
from the bounty of bush and tree
of sea and ocean
their riches still unfolding
for our every need:
To these riches I say
"L'CHAYIM!"

    L'Chayim
    to all the creatures of the world,
    to bird and beast
    to every insect
    that wants to live

I say "L'Chayim"
to the young
to the new-born baby
crying at birth
to old men and women
clinging to life

But most of all
I say
"L'Chayim"
to the kindly men and women
who lend a shoulder

spread forth their hands
give of self
knowing we are all part
of this earth, this world
this life

"L'CHAYIM"

Good Yom Tov

Good Yom Tov!
You hear these words
and they are like a golden ring
encircling your heart,
like the roundness of the challa
and the sweetness of honey

Friends, neighbors, dear ones!
Take time
to send your greetings,
your messages of love:
for otherwise
there is no holiday

On The Day Of The Bar-Mitzvah

There is an awesome hush
in the temple
on the day
of the Bar-Mitzvah

A soft ray of light
filters in through the window
and rests on you,
drawing our gaze to you
magnetically

Your voice rings clearly,
melodiously,
as you sway to the chant
of the prayers;
and our hearts ache
with nameless joys,
with nameless sorrows

Stand proudly, my son,
seed of generations past,
flower of love,
symbol of man's goodness
Proclaim your faith
in the faith of your fathers

Forget not the everlasting
devotion and love
of your Mother,
nor of all the women of Israel,

who are ever watchful, zealous,
for our children

Wear with joy, my son,
your new tallis
and satin yarmelka

Remember the Torah
before which you stand,
the Rabbi's hand
on your shoulder,
his blessing, his words

Today you are a son
unto the people of Israel!

To A Small Boy Lighting
A Chanukah Candle

You stand still
before the Menorah,
your little hand holding
a thin blue candle
its tiny light's
flickering, flickering,
reflected in your
solemn eyes

The yarmelka now covers
your entire head,
but a few curls fall
on your baby forehead

As the years pass,
your world will change
you will travel swiftly,
not only spanning
the four corners
of the earth,
but reaching dazzling planets,
new heights,
new worlds

As, yes,
every man yearns
to touch a star!
But remember, child,
this simple thing —
wherever you may be,
light a candle
at Chanukah time

A Child's Seder

The young bride
proudly
embroidered
her husband's initials
on the white satin and lace
matzo cover,
and the years mellowed
it to a deep gold.
The children love
to eat the matzo
from its soft folds

They love the
delicate wine glasses
shining on the Seder table;
they love the sweet red wine,
the Pesach food;
the Charoses,
and even the Maror
and Karpos

The house is filled
with laughter and happiness
and the children
doze dreamily
on the night
of the Seder
as they listen
to their father
tell the story of Moses

and the slaves;
over and over again
they hear the word
freedom
freedom
freedom

Young Rabbi

He speaks,
not soothingly, nor placatingly,
but rather with the accurate
incision of a surgeon
probing, analyzing, dissecting
till truth is revealed,
sometimes stark, comfortless,
yet the truth
clear-cut, unadorned
in all its simplicity

He speaks,
his slate-grey eyes make no
compromise
even with those who plead for
comfort,
even with those who do not wish
age-old thoughts disturbed,
but like the ancient prophets,
he harangues his people
and teaches them with taut-wire
firmness,
because he loves them

Pesach

Oh
let us sit
at the Seder table
together
once again
this year

Let us rejoice
in our freedom
for which so many perished
and suffered
let us never forget them

Let us remember
those we loved
and still love
and join in prayer,
song and food,
in unity and
harmony and peace,
as one small sign
of our humanity
and remembrance
and reverence

Yom Kippur Scene

Everyone was in the temple
on Yom Kippur,
and a grandfather came
with his little grandson
old man, little boy,
sitting closely together

And when the Ark was opened,
and the congregation rose as one,
quietly,
the old man
lifted the little boy
to see the Ark

Suddenly, with the sharp,
piercing cry of the Shofar,
the child's head
fell on the old man's shoulder,
first from fear
then he lifted his face
and stared

And the child did not understand,
but he listened
to the music that touched
your very vitals
and he didn't say a word
but you knew, watching him,
that the little boy would never forget
this day with his grandfather in Shule
on the day of Yom Kippur

Rosh Hashanah I

I

While all of us celebrate
and rejoice in this
beautiful holiday,
you will not be there

While all of us
greet our family
sit together
sing together
listen to the chanting
of cantor and choir,
the rabbi's sermon,
you will not be there

You will have your donut and coffee,
read the business page,
the baseball news,
you will rush again
on this Holy Day
and your music will be
the ringing of the cash register,
and at night you will automatically
turn the knob of your TV

II

Oh, I plead with you
Not today!
Not this year! א

Come to the Synagogue
listen to the ancient music
words
carried through the current of
                        centuries
never lost
through bloodshed, martyrdom, death

Dear one,
come to Shule
sit with us
the thread of remembrance
has never left
it can never leave
except a scar, an emptiness

Dear one, do not hesitate
do not turn away
we will greet you
as a beloved brother
we both will start anew
we both will be renewed

Rosh Hashanah II

What moved me this morning
the prayers?
the music?
the breathing   crying sounds
cascading
enveloping
the congregation?

It was a simple thing

Walking slowly
down the aisle
a young man,
perhaps a grandson,
gently guiding
an elderly woman
who held his arm
proudly

Queen Esther

Esther
Beautiful Queen
You will always shine in our lives,
our favorite heroine
As children we happily
heard the story of Purim

      Glorious Queen Esther
      the best part is the happy ending
      Despite all obstacles
      you won freedom
      for our people

      Is it any wonder then
      that we have great heroines,
      so many unsung,
      who gave their lives
      for others?

The Shofar

The Shofar's sounds
are loud and piercing
and we remember
its warning
its frightening reminder
not to sin
not to criticize
not to be foolish
or cruel
and more and more

> The sounds
> linger more faintly
> between the New Years

What sound or word
will stay with us
in the coming year?

Chanukah Time — 1961

Not all at once
are the candles lighted,
but one more each time:
and so it is
the more candles we light,
the less there will be
darkness

Slowly, patiently we will wait
till all the candles gleam
with love and understanding
with sharing and listening
with seeking and learning
and if we must
like the Maccabees,
with fighting

This Story

Yes, my children
I have a wonderful gift
for you for Chanukah

Is it money?
        No

Is it something to wear?
A ring or pearls?
Is it something to eat?
        No

I will give you, this Chanukah,
the old old story
of the immortal
Maccabees

I will tell you of their mission,
their battle
for more than freedom,
for their very life and soul,
for right above all else
and the gift they struggled to attain
is prized above all else
by all men

Yes, my children
the story of the Maccabees
is my gift
to which no other can compare

The Blessing

Then comes the final moment
the rabbi stands
with hands held high
and blesses us

Our eyes glisten with tears
our hearts beat
to the metronome of memories

In that instant
we are related to all Jews
past and present
who stand thus
waiting to be blessed

Tribute To A Rabbi

It is not you alone we hear
when you utter songs of praise
for that which is true
and wondrous in the world,
for even one simple word
inspiring one human being,
for one simple act that warms
a fellow-man

It is not you alone we hear
when your voice
is torn with pain and scorn
for the greedy, malicious,
and for the greatest
enemies of all:
the ignorant who will not listen,
the indifferent who do not care

It is not you alone who brings
to Judaism spark and fire,
light and energy:
to hew a path,
to ease a burden,
to teach and guide,
to help and heal,
it is not you alone

Embodied in your spirit,
emblazoned in your heart,
etched in every fibre of your being,

are the leaf and twig and branch
the grain, the life and breath,
of all our sages,
all our prophets,
spun and woven
with blood and prayer
through the ages

Kaddish

With the words
"Let those who mourn
now rise,"
·it is still in the synagogue
You rise
and stand,
head bowed,
limbs trembling,
overcome with weakness,
longing, grief
for that one
whom you loved
more than anything
God created

    And as you whisper
    the Kaddish,
    repeating the
    Hebrew phrases,
    there is no
    word of consolation,
    no attitude of pity,
    yet you are poignantly aware
    of all those
    beside you
    who sit
    with tear-filled eyes
    and aching hearts
    like yours

Shalom

Wide wide
we open our arms
to welcome you,
all who need us
all who come to us,
never to circle for a landing
never to founder in ships
never to wander
Here, here is your haven

Those saved from the branding fire
those rescued from the choking fumes
those wrested from the camps of hell,
you are our cherished ones
to you we fling open our arms

We will heal your wounds,
our waters, cool and sweet and fresh,
are waiting to soothe your weariness,
our songs will gladden your ears
and awaken your soul,
our hands will hold yours
with the promise of brotherhood,
our hearts will pray for you

    All Israel,
    everyone
    in every corner,
    street, avenue,
    every tree and stone

will proclaim its welcome to you,
long-awaited brother, sister
father, mother, child

In place of fire and hate
you will have benevolence,
in place of ashes and blood
you will have trees laden
with the sweetest fruit

Here all the good of the old
will be retained
and the tragic erased
and here, high in the sky,
our light will flash,
transmitting its power,
its message to all

No precious jewels can
gleam as bright
as the beam of the Eternal Light
saying over and over
Shalom Shalom

Know My People

Know my people
learn about them
who they are
where they come from
what they believe
what they think
what they do

    Know my people
    their fathers
    and grandfathers
    ah their mothers
    and grandmothers too

Learn about these people
from the days of the Bible
onward to all the countries
they trod
where they always learned,
rarely forsaking
the wisdom they inherited
and guarded with their very lives

There is no stereotype!
They come from many lands,
speaking many tongues
there are statesmen
doctors lawyers scientists
singers and musicians
teachers actors writers

everywhere you will find them,
my people . . .
they are fearless,
why should they fear other men?

They are human beings
who are not always right
but they seek the light
Do not try to lead them like sheep,
they will not follow blindly,
but show them kindness and understanding
and they will take you to their hearts

Know my people
salute them
for their vision,
the poetry of their writings,
the depth of their knowledge
and creativity

Know my people
the sons and daughters
of Abraham, Isaac and Jacob,
who have not forsaken their fathers
nor ever will

Mamme-Loshen

His English
is impeccable
the words strung together
like a brilliant spectacle:
But what gives him pleasure
and his listeners hanoah?
A Yiddish joke, of course!

He lovingly elaborates
every point
rolling the words round his tongue
like some mychel,
his eyes twinkling
his lips wide with laughter
his hands helping form the picture
of the mysah
with the grace of a dancer
the creativity
of a sculptor
or artist

His audience wants more, more
their faces say
"It's such a mechiah
to listen to him"
and their faces
are like babies'
snuggling up
to mother
who used to croon

a lullaby
in
Mamme-Loshen
forever sweet to their ears
forever memorable
forever loved

When You Ask A Jew

People ask:
Why does a Jew answer
a question with a question?

Always the Jew asks questions,
this is his nature,
he wants to know why,
he is always looking for
hidden meanings,
hidden shadings,
he probes,
he seeks
he knows the smallest thing
can be the greatest mystery
he explores,
he leaves nothing unturned,
he is not satisfed
till he has the answer
to his question

All the descendants
of the first seekers,
the first leaders,
the first thinkers,
bear this mark
this distinction
You will find them
in the laboratories
and the universities
they are everywhere,

delighting in the quest
in the adventure
of living

The history of his life
never ceases to intrigue him,
the stories of his people
are treasured
and repeated
and always there is the question
that needs an answer,
why did this happen
what does it mean
what can you learn
from this miracle
this tragedy
this experience

And when you ask
a Jew,
why do you answer
a question with a question
he smiles
and asks:
"WHY NOT?"

People Of The Book

Who else but a Jew
would stand up
to honor the Torah,
Book of Books

During the High Holy Days
he rises
as the rabbi and cantor
march down the aisle
holding the precious Scroll

He is overcome with awe
when his fingers touch
this Book

Each time he reads it
he finds new meaning, insight
though old, it is ever new

This Book is a vital
living entity,
holy, revered,
sometimes paraded through the streets
for all to see
to glorify

A special holiday, Simchas Torah,
proclaims the pride
of those
to whom the Torah

is the pinnacle
of light and truth,
their reason for living

Book of mystery
Book of miracles
Book that teaches and heals
Book that scolds and denounces
Book filled with strange stories
we are bound to you

The Yad

Many hands have held you,
the hands of scholars
and the hands
of the very young,
pointing reverently
at the Hebrew script

> It is as if
> you were a symbol
> divinely guided
> pointing the way,
> the direction

What better compass
for a Jew
than the Yad
focusing,
stressing
each word and phrase
and thought
of the Torah

The old men's voices
quaver with awe
and the young ones'
quiver with wonder,
sensing the spiritual
affinity with those who
have held and will hold
the Yad

All These Prayers

Rabbi,
aren't we asking
too much of the Lord?
you call on him
so often
and you speak
with such kovid
so much faith,
with such praise

Rabbi, you know what?
I am embarrassed . . .
all these prayers
exhortations
paeans,
from every corner
of the earth,
from such a babel
of tongues

and I sit quietly
in the synagogue

Lerer

Never wavering,
never faltering,
never halting,
our Lerer
for so many decades
spoke the words
to boy and girl
that buoyed them up
and lifted them
higher and higher
in the stratum
of learning

Baked into our souls,
burned into our beings,
are the precepts,
the ideas and thoughts,
the places and people,
the books and songs,
that our Lerer
brought to us
with fire and love
and with faith
that some day,
somehow,
we too will leave
our mark on others

How Long Will You Wait?

How long will you wait,
my people?
How long will you sit still,
how long?
How long will it be
before you hear the voices
of your brothers,
choked and torn
with suffering,
lifeless . . . loveless? ·

Perhaps you cannot see them:
perhaps you cannot see their eyes,
dead with the death of despair,
perhaps you cannot see their faces
barren of hope,
beaten, blank,
black:
tear-stained as the earth
when too much rain has fallen

Listen then, my people!
Do you hear?
Listen!
Have you forgotten?
These are the voices
of your brothers,
calling, pleading,
crying for your hand,
begging for your help!

Speak, my people,
speak with love and kinship
to those who call,
with pride and firmness
to their enemies

Unite, my people, unite!
hands clasping,
arms entwined,
shoulder to shoulder,
there will be strength!
Hope!
Success!

Fight, my people, fight!
If there be no other way;
if only the weapon
will strike with fear
our enemies!
Fight, fight
even if blood must flow!

Act, my people, act!
Give your strength,
your energy,
your wealth!
Give with all your heart!
Give with all your soul!

How long can you wait?
How long can you sit still?

To A Boy Away From Home

We think of you
we pray for you
our hearts
yearn for you
and yet we knew
you had to go

We knew you had to go,
depart from home and family
and yet there is such comfort
for you are in Israel
you are home in Israel
this too is your home

And I Am Proud

I walk on different paths
I taste I see I hear
I think I love
But I cannot tear myself away
from you, my people

> When I hear the sound
> of ancient music
> or see your faces,
> it is
> a well of memories
> from the days of old
> to these times

It is the super-human valor
of my people
that rises
clear and pure and certain
. . . and I am proud

Never Again

They walk in shock
and disbelief
that any human being can honor
the killers
of so many people

How can their monstrous acts
be forgotten
or forgiven

The cream of our people
tortured and slain,
disfigured,
crippled
these will be forever remembered
forever mourned

The history of murder
must never again
repeat itself

You cannot create reconciliation
by force
upon those who still bear
the anguish and marks
of their suffering
and humiliation

The words *Never Again*
are stamped in our hearts
and we remember

Lament

For the Eleven Israeli Athletes who were murdered at the Olympic Games in Munich

The Memorial Service
in Israel
tears
your
heart

the mind is shattered
with grief
and horror

How many times
have we sobbed
at the El Mole Rachamin
how many years
has this Prayer
been rendered
for Jewish martyrs

But what is our shock
compared
to the Mothers
and Fathers
and Family
of the zestful young athletes
wrest from life by madmen

No one
can
ever
replace

these beautiful young people,
no prayer can ever
probe the depth
of despair
at their loss

No recompense
no retaliation
can erase the searing pain
or bring them back
again

So Many

I prayed
and You did not hear me,
I cried
but You did not see my tears

How can I believe again?
How can I hope?

And there are so
many like me,
so many

For Those Who Do Not Care

You turn your head
and walk away
when someone talks about
Auschwitz or Dachau . . .
You do not care

      You who shout for freedom
      in your life,
      think about all those
      who came before you
      in your family,
      in your country,
      Where does your freedom
      come from?

And do not turn your head
and do not walk away

      Evil strikes with speed
      to crush
      to cripple
      to exterminate
      and it turns its head
      and walks away

Petition

I don't mind sighing, Lord,
and I don't mind crying
but let my sighs be sighs of bliss
and let my tears
be tears of joy

Let my eyes reflect delight
let my thoughts be filled with light
let my words be a caress
oh, lift my hand to heal and bless

The Old Candlesticks

The old candlesticks are on the table,
it is Shabbos
and they stand as a reminder
of my prayers,
of the tears down my cheeks,
of my thanks
for all the good
bestowed upon us

They know the secret
longings of my heart,
they know the story
of our lives,
they heard the
singing of the Kiddush
by childish voices,
and the sound of laughter

Week after week they stand
like loyal members of the family,
always ready to burn brightly
on Shabbos

Tree Of Life

Dedicated to Deon Simon

This seed
you planted,
do not worry or fret
over it
it will bear fruit
its scent will be sweeter
than any rose

This seed you planted
will grow
like wisdom
like love
like hope
like faith,
stronger and stronger
will be its fruit,
overflowing will be its harvest

Our tears have watered it
the light of our love has been its sun
we have shielded it
with our very life
we have nourished it
with every breath
every drop of blood

This seed?
it has the time of all eternity:
wait
be still
and know

If Only

"I am reconciled to death,"
she said,
her face white,
her voice resigned,
as if those words
came after many struggles.
much pain

But oh
if only
she would be
RECONCILED TO LIFE!

Where Else

They wanted to entertain him,
the man who was saved
from the holocaust

They wanted to show him
all the wonders of L.A.

But in a few words
he told them
what he wanted to see,
where he wanted to be

"First," he said
with a big smile,
as if to say where else?
"Nem mich
tzu die
Yiddishe gahs."

Controversy

He went to Bitberg
to lay a wreath
at the cemetery
of nazi soldiers

But forgot
the millions
who lost their lives
and the endless emptiness
of those who lost them

Oh where is the wreath
at the concentration camps
for the buried and burned
and discarded

Scars and numbers
stamped on human flesh
do not fade away

More tragic than that,
the soul is seared forever.
Ah, no, a wreath is not enough
NOT ENOUGH

Am Yisroel Chai

The auditorium is packed with people
young and old, sitting shoulder to shoulder
their faces pale, sorrowful
for their lost . . .
their breath is like
a stifled sigh,
heavy with sadness
and the strain of
tears held back too long

> Their eyes burn
> like a thousand Yahrzeit lamps
> as the Six Candles are lighted
> and their ears ache
> to the strains of the El Mole Rachamin

The Cantor's voice
hurts us and cuts us
with his plaintive lamentations
as the survivors of concentration camps
stand mutely listening

> There is no hatred here,
> only the crushed and wordless
> sense of shame
> for those who should have acted but did not
> for those who should have spoken but were silent

And as the tall white candles burn
and the flags of our countries

stand guard,
an old man rises on the stage
to speak:
Our pulse quickens
at his passion —
With lifted fist
he prophecies:
"My beloved brothers and sisters:
   AM YISROEL CHAI!"